Consolation Miracle

Crab Orchard Award Series in Poetry

First Book Award

Consolation Miracle

CHAD DAVIDSON

Crab Orchard Review &

Southern Illinois University Press

Carbondale

Printed in the United States of America

06   05   4   3

The Crab Orchard Award Series in Poetry is a joint publishing
venture of Southern Illinois University Press and *Crab Orchard
Review.* This series has been made possible by the generous support
of the Office of the President of Southern Illinois University and the
Office of the Vice Chancellor for Academic Affairs and Provost at
Southern Illinois University Carbondale.

**Crab Orchard Award Series in Poetry Editor: Jon Tribble
Judge for 2002: Rodney Jones**

Library of Congress Cataloging-in-Publication Data

Davidson, Chad, 1970–
   Consolation miracle / Chad Davidson.
   p. c.m. — (Crab Orchard award series in poetry)
   I. Title. II. Series.
PS3604 .A946C655 2003
813'.6—dc21
ISBN 0-8093-2541-1   2003002088

Printed on recycled paper.

The paper used in this publication meets the minimum
requirements of American National Standard for Information
Sciences—Permanence of Paper for Printed Library Materials,
ANSI Z39.48-1992. ∞

FOR GWEN

Contented with such random consolations
As the wind deposits
In slithered and too ample pockets.
  —Hart Crane, "Chaplinesque"

. . . My crumb
my mansion . . .
  —Elizabeth Bishop, "A Miracle for Breakfast"

Contents

FIVE

Acknowledgments

Grateful acknowledgment is made to the editors of the following publications, in which poems from this book originally appeared, though sometimes in slightly different form:

American Literary Review—"A" and "To My Left Ear Canal, Deformed at Birth"

Cimarron Review—"All the Ashtrays in Rome"

Colorado Review—"Two Crows"

Crab Orchard Review—"Mushrooms," "The Pear," and "Virtus Dormitiva"

DoubleTake—"Cockroaches: Ars Poetica"

Iron Horse Literary Review—"The Contents of Abraham Lincoln's Pockets"

Mid-American Review—"This Is the Cow"

Nashville Scene—"The Scarecrow Odes"

New Delta Review—"The Floating World"

Notre Dame Review—"People Who Jump off Cliffs"

The Paris Review—"Cleopatra's Bra" and "The Last Decade of the Fifteenth Century"

Passages North—"Bite Your Tongue" and "Space"

Pequod—"Ending"

Poet Lore—"Alchemy" and "The *Kama Sutra*'s Banished Illustrator"

Seattle Review—"Starfish"

Seneca Review—"Scratched Retina: Memento Mori"

32 Poems—"Boxes" and "The Match"

"Space" was published as a limited-edition leaflet by Poggibonsi Press, 2003.

"All the Ashtrays in Rome," "Cleopatra's Bra," "The Contents of Abraham Lincoln's Pockets," "Ending," "The Last Decade of the Fifteenth Century," and "To My Left Ear Canal, Deformed at Birth" (under the title "Gently Pressing a Deformed Ear to the Wall in St. Mark's") were published in a limited-edition chapbook entitled *Tourist Guide to the Forgotten City* by Trilobite Press, 2003.

Thanks to the Rotary Ambassadorial Scholarship Committee and the Constance Saltonstall Foundation for the Arts, whose generous support allowed me time to work on this book in ideal settings. Special thanks to Bruce Bond, B. H. Fairchild, Austin Hummell, and John Vernon, teachers as well as friends, for their wisdom and instruction. Praise to my family, especially my mother. And my deepest appreciation and gratitude to John Poch, without whose friendship and advice this book would never have existed.

Consolation Miracle

A

Today, you see only the letter *a* when you read. All other letters fall away—the pouting *y*, the disconcerted *r*, the liquids caught inside the concave *u*—all gone in the absolute *a*. In Hebrew, the first letter of the alphabet is aleph, as is the Greek alpha. In school, large apples hang on walls, a giant *A* bright red. Red is the color of *a* rushing into your first words, barbaric and without shame, stamped as it is on report cards and meat.

Pin it to an adulterer's blouse. Shout it as you careen into the rocks, or just before. Or when you rise out of bed at night in sweat, knowing only what you dreamed was so elemental you have no word. An apple a day keeps the doctor away. Apple an and away. And your apple falls away from the page that stays the way it's able, that lies there, lies to you.

Allah, Adam, Ariel. Every time you form your mouth around the *a*-ness of the *a*, or listen to a newborn learn its name, or a poet from A.D., when *and* becomes *a*, and *catatonic* becomes *aa*, and *aardvark* becomes *aaa*, and *and and* becomes *a a*—when all the words bow down and lift up their sails to the wind of your voice, your gift to the wind and the world you're in, your stars, your names for God—say *a*, say *a*. Say *a*, because one day, one by one, they will disappear, leave the page, your head, and the silent, infant world. Once there was *a*.

One

Starfish

Such brilliant boredom under the sun.
How they carve shadows in the moon-

dust of the ocean floor, each arm
radiant, excruciating

to the thousand hungry mouths
they tease: small wonder

we try to thank them. Lucky ones
in tanks in low lit city aquariums,

or those desiccated on the shore—
in time we find these stars

more precious than what we count on.
Orbiting in glass skies

foreign to their silences, we puzzle
over their power to regenerate,

how the stories their bodies make
replay. In Hollywood,

we walk their silhouettes, unaware
how they fell there. Seeing stars

over the infant—they swing
from cribposts in primordial dark.

Odd angels thrown into a fire
of coastlines crowned with bodies,

and which of us could rip their wings
in greed, demystify them,

break our promise to continue
with these myths we made,

sunk in constellations
we guide our lives by?

Mushrooms

Under the lazy lip of the oyster
coated in loam, the porcino,
or lowly morel, laymushroom—

here and there the pink
gills that kill, and will we know
the difference in the woods?

Ushered into their musky rooms,
we come to expect their place
at our tables, forked and rising,

the closest thing we have
to edible encomium.
We make them half brothers

to the skull, because to stare
that hard at anything begins
the slow mutation—what some buried

part of us believes will never come.
If we depend on the fleshy zero
of their caps, so much is nothing

more than beauty wrapped
in night's clothes. Come morning
they greet us: the slow bough

of the pileus, umbrellas reigning
over the tiny ones as yet unworthy.
Concentrating, we sense our own bodies

hidden there, or forced up through
that crevice just above metabolism, say,
welling up in the warmth of the palate.

The Yawn

Boredom. Yet science does nothing for me.
No consolation. I'm tired of poetry,
though I know the fear a yawn
once inspired, like the swan

at the edge of the lake by our house:
how it darts away from us
just as we're close enough to grab
it, how the yawn used to stab

us in the back that way, the soul
rising right after birth. The old
science of the yawn as phantasm:
like Greek myth or orgasm,

somehow too fulfilling to be
painful. Yet the jaw falls,
Icarine, tragic. The call
Orphic, out of a need to see

down the throat the frail balloon
lungs paired off and abloom.
Or how I throw myself out
of sleep. Opening a stout

night's end with my eyes
squeezing, I look in the mirror,
witness myself eating air,
agasp, my daily chance to gaze

into this face's oldest pain,
more than some mute renegade
wail, this tooth-jeweled grenade
thrown out of the well again.

A Hand

Still I trust enough, would give it away
to anyone who asks. To a cellist,
say, whose own hand is proof the mind
still loves its animals flitting about
under a floodlight's stare. And among ours,
which but the most fearful wouldn't rise
up before the encore to beat its twin?
Such faithlessness, itself a backhanded
hope, or hope's photo-negative.
For a hand houses the most opposable
of views, its flare for pleasing fingering
into the darkest glove, air duct, rat hole.
You've seen this. How a hand skates around
the orbitals in de la Tour's nocturnes:
it could fuse a skull's soft spot, the least human
of human. And that finger of flame peering
over the frontal ridge? Some days our hands
are scarcely more than such beacons, waving
to others like them, handy in a crowd.

We deserve at least one. Improperly
supervised, though, it's true: a bad hand
can crack a book spine or, worse, kill
a good night's sleep falling asleep under
the body rooted at its end. That's when
the deal comes strangest to us, an arrival
from the least of our tremblings through a shower
of nerves. Awaking, we've even felt the gates
open, the blood returning to its canals
through the palm's basin open and cradling
the last thing it knew by heft and contour.
And for all its grabbing, who wants one stiff,
or limp as a fish? Almost blind, one reaches
for another, as if they were parents fresh
and clumsy enough to hand down all we want.

The Contents of Abraham Lincoln's Pockets

As calmly as a hand will shake
another after shooting a gun,
a Skylark bends around a pole.
As spectator, you can't remember
why you speed toward Dallas, strangling
a cell phone with your free hand.

My God, the way we arrange our time
you'd think we were born to die,
that time was endless, at least enough
to visit a museum. I'm sure
the driver never realized the pole
would be the last thing he'd rush into.

And like a thrush rushing itself
in the windshield in the dead
of summer, you're still inventing
the final seconds, the act that shakes
the stage like a dying man's hand
pocketward for the old

timepiece, as if this time
were retrievable, at least
compatible with all its pieces:
a wallet, some summer snapshots
byzantine in posture, stubs
for Mavericks, Stars. And in a sense,

we're all stars in our own museums.
To lessen death by dying? This
is why we love spectacles.
The better to see ourselves.
And like the thrush waiting to rush
the glass, we're here: in the pocket

of time before the bomb or shot
that forces the hands to beat themselves
senseless, as if pockets swallowed
our hands instead of arming them.

To My Left Ear Canal, Deformed at Birth

Flitting like a coal bird
in a kiddie pool in a blocked-off cul de sac,
this is my heart questioning

as dog whistles and quarantined ships do.
Take my brain, how it fires
its audibles to whatever deaf gondolier

is in the blood, battering
my Bridge of Sighs. Plunging into fleshy
shores or piercing old

wood gates as you round the wound
and write it off, you
might as well be Saint Mark, blame

graverobbers and God
for losing your hair, your hearing. All canals end
at this tomb, my head,

flooded each year. Can't you appreciate this thump
mosaic of doors,
and how closely Venice sounds to Virginia

coaling up its sepulcher?
You are a door cracked open to the ocean
far from Venice.

And if ever two were meant to be earful
of the world, it is you and I.
Please let this silence turn negotiable.

Listening is punishment,
and people are being drowned, so block this ear
and sing. Block and sing.

Block off the canal and sing like a dirty bird.

Two

The Match

The burner and the blackout crave you: pilot
of heat, purveyor of the innocent
candle and cigarette, light we tame
to tame the night. Cupped, inviolate,
a winter moth or prayer we never sent
away, you live in seconds what we name
a life. A sudden cleansing, you Prometheus
come as toothpick, the false fire lent
to our fingertips, lightbulb of the lame
idea: may your phosphorus forgive us,
old flame.

Alchemy

I hammered out a love affair with you
in New Orleans. Your name was Lydia.
We bedded in Algiers and staggered through
each night of three like Goths in Scythia,
unwelcomed, unafraid. We were lustrous
in our sex, each night of three, coving
out of the black the name we gave you: *mistress.*
Though unmarried, I felt guilt in loving
so coldly, spellbound on a mindless bed.
When we ferried to the quarter on noon-
time runs, we clenched the steel rails, the dead
weight of the craft. No kiss. No talk. No june-
bug buzz, but silence, approaching summer and all
the quarter was: the foil, the coming fall.

The Floating World

In a movie on the floating world,
I watch the way the Japanese drew union:
swan-legged, the exclamatic O

of the vagina, and how the men climbed on,
arched, lips protruding for a kiss,
eyes drawn tight. I've always been impressed

with Eastern subtlety, the thin horse-hair
brush and rice paper feel of the parchment
as if it could all melt in the mouth.

Surely that was thought of. There in the parlor,
the white legs of a geisha wound in cloth,
fans unfolding. The camera cranes, pulls

her strapped hair into focus as voiceovers
wonder how the Japanese distinguished
love from art, or if such lines existed,

or exist. Then we pan to the bonsai,
trained, pruned to fold inward. And the geisha,
tethered to her art, as if painted there.

The *Kama Sutra*'s Banished Illustrator

I only drew the woman. Raised cheekbones
curving impossibly in my hand, the slender
neck, hair pulled back like rope: all

female after brushing the vagina's conch
with agni. I shaded with my stained finger
around the breasts; gave her arms, karma.

Her pupils swelled, anticipating the loss.
How I coveted the way she seemed
to stare at my palm while I labored, my subject.

Any artist will tell you they're not easy,
the eyes; I ground them into reflection.
She never saw past the image I gave her,

just as I could not stop scorching her skin
with reds and ochres saved for Brahma's eyes.
A flame of curry stained her mouth's rim.

Here, a hand rose for wine a lover brings.
His name would well up in her parched throat.
Before the night, she would accept him again,

whom I refused to draw. It was a trick
to make ecstasy—the floating legs,
head tossed back, the half-eaten plum—

contrary to her leisure. In fact I stole
my sketches long before I finished,
before she bled back into my hands.

Almost Ending with a Troubadour Line

You call and, almost singing, say Manet
is on TV, his lewd *Olympia*.
And without words we fall synchronized
down the nude, with you, a day away,
breathing lightly in my ear. Absentia
of the phone, of this painting, the eyes
of some Manet and you peer from a terrace
lording over this city and its dementia,
where a hundred blushing TVs spy,
where neither song nor hawthorn flower please
me: please.

The Pear

The constancy of flesh will drive us,
how this pome ascends the stairs
to its origin. A boy shakes

pears down off the higher branches
as his friends scavenge underneath,
groping for the tapered necks.

If we find ourselves holding them,
hungry, if that's the word,
then we are testament

to what festers in their fattened lobes
like a ball of sugar bees.
Here is Augustine, his thin

fingers tearing into skin
that barely holds the pulp
around its core. Poised nudes

forever in their sunny chairs,
they await whatever plucking
comes. When they're eaten

with darkness plunging
always farther into their hearts,
a few seeds ache then swell black

as appetite. Or as their profile
imitates a lover's pendant
breasts, we take them in

as we do our own bodies,
as infants do, wanting anything
to give our wanting form.

Cleopatra's Bra

It is one thing to uphold one's passions,
another to retain them. That thin seam
between impassioned and fashion: it could be

just another form of governing,
intimacy. Who knows if sequins spiraled
around each nipple, lapis clinging to straps.

Each mouthful of wine would raise her body heat
until a touch of gold slivered and rose
off her dark skin, caught somewhere

in a jewel of sweat. This is the Egypt
I imagine: pyramids, obelisks,
the Valley of Kings, and one torn bra.

Meanwhile, the Romans fashioned their parchment,
filled it with long strings of letters: *a*
for *ave, b* for *beato* (blessed), *c,*

of course, for *Caesar,* with no space between,
as to appear infinite. Augustus did try.
The old argument: *come home, she's bad news.*

But for Antony there would be no empire
cloven: a pregnant dream as he lay
again with her, clothes strewn on the ground

like artifacts of a forgotten city
under ash, and those two bodies caught
once more, together, for all of Rome to see.

Because it did end, Virgil says, in ruins
of a city, toppled towers, and one
fictitious Dido who let it all hang out

one Carthage summer so hot the oarsmen
gave up their fears, Acestes descended his throne
without bearskin, Aeneas loved and left,

Dido died. I like to imagine her scrawling
a message to the future regarding love—
flagrant love—and sacrificial fires

like those she clothed her city in one night:
Beware the Roman come to lie with you,
one hand heart-heavy and bound there

like the swearing-in of a city
official. Feeling her lover fiddle
with the clasp, Cleopatra must have thought,

does everything come undone with this
one small breach of virtue? One giant step
backward, she hears the inevitable

unleashing of the dogs, the centuries
head to toe in armor, and the lift,
they say, of a shallow wicker basket.

I like to imagine her calmly spreading
her robe, a leisurely cup of wine,
her fingers unclasping the bra from behind

as the asp negotiates the sea
of azure silk that separates them, empires
colliding, and the golden tint of scales.

Three

This Is the Cow

She must be milked every morning so that she will produce milk, and the milk
must be boiled in order to be mixed with coffee to make coffee and milk.
    —García Márquez, *One Hundred Years of Solitude*

Imagine the years being sucked out
of you, the losses so numerous
you count gains instead: the shiver

of holy water, your quinceañera,
burnt cedar, the faith in the cross-
town taxi in Mexico, not knowing *derecha*

from *izquierda*. Think of all the shattered
glasses cursing the sky, the women you keep
yearning for. You taste the slow arrival

of the moment only to watch it fade
anxiously. Now think of absence, staring
at some beast in a field and saying *never*

have I seen this thing in front of me.
Then the cow moos, and you understand
the simple lexicon of the green

in its mouth, the dynamics of the jaw like
nothing you can't recall, have never seen.
And what impossible eyes—unlike yours—

swelling with your losses and successes.
They too are losses, ready to escape
your skin like the sweets of a piñata,

the dull thud of the instant still there,
when you realize that to know this beast
by name is to lose this beast, lose it

hopelessly in the catacombs
of names for other things: the *coffee bean,*
your *blood,* the ripe *guava, penitence,*

the left bank of *the river,* crumbling,
where you learned *cow* from awkward profile,
milk-heavy, its one eye, reflecting.

Bite Your Tongue

Bullets are for movie stars and going
cold turkey. Nails are for something
close to fear. Though I've felt teeth kick up

like gravel on the tongue's underbelly.
Tongue-tied I kept the mordant pleasure
to myself. Speak in tongues, but bite

your tongue when you have spoken too much.
As in *Double Indemnity.* My favorite line
is *shut up, baby:* bold, recalcitrant boredom

in black and white. Or the clink of ice
in a highball gin, what another
drink always means: something close

to fear. There must have been that mean gray
time between the silents and the talkies
when the face meant less, the tongue more.

One night, the world went to bed with no voice.
It must have seemed a miracle, and so real,
that reel of tape unraveling on its spool

like the tongue of a woman hot
from liquor and her bald, snoozing husband.
Or in my favorite cartoon, the dead man speaks

in pure idiom. Naturally, each cat
owns another's tongue, lays it paw-wide,
flat and vascular even in those days

of heavy color saturation. Tongueless
was the trait, *shut up baby* the safest
insult to yourself. But say we all

kept on in silence as pictures spoke
through the lips of every Jack and Jill
who could afford the matinee. News

hummed into allied bombings, films
went noir. Even as we could, we talked
less. And when the tongue shrinks inside

the skull, looks less a wick than a bad worm,
and candles blow out for a new century,
we'll peer from the balcony at mimes

performing wars that never started and say,
what strange sounds their stomachs make, their feet,
the purrs from their tired, flapping arms.

Boxes

I invent a boy who plays with boxes
down the street. He grieves, and I can't help
but think of Lazarus whom he coaxes
from the tomb propped on cardboard pulp
and chicken wire. Behind him three dark spires
display the sky in splinters. I've come to this
poem. It is a box. The page admires
how these lines swell into a cross-
hatch of words turned dirge. I swear I never
knew this boy. And Lazarus is a present.
Unwrap him and he'll fly. Why be tethered
to the church? Poem, I resent
your putting boxes inside boxes. Don't
call me if the church opens.
                                        Let's be blunt:
I stole the image of the box from a friend.
I put it in two sonnets I keep running
up against. Lines summon their own end,
and the boy now has a balloon. Stunning
how it looks against the worn shade,
the brown of the churchstones. The box waits
like an empty tomb: Lazarus made
whole again. A voiceover begins: It is late
one April afternoon. A typical town
by all respects. The church turns under a flight
of clouds balloonlike. The boy who coaxes
the balloon along hears his own
voice then say *rise, rise, rise*. The light
flicks on. It's over. The boy is in his box.

Cockroaches: Ars Poetica

They know that death is merely of the body
not the species, know their putrid chitin
is always memorable. We call them ugly
with their blackened exoskeletons,
their wall-crawlings as we paw at them.
Extreme adaptability, we say.
And where there's one there's probably a million
more who lie and laugh in cracks close by.
At first they seem so pitiful and base
feeding on what we leave behind. Content
to watch us watching them, their hidden grace
is endless procreation: it keeps them constant,
believing they'll live to read our requiem
with the godlike eyes we used to look at them.

Two Crows

Three crows
huddling between telephone wires
is not a metaphor. Depravity is exquisite

in the one
huddling between the search
for carrion and the carrion it last remembers,

reminding the others
of carrion: black matted
feathers, eyes falling inward. I want to know

if crows bleed
from their eyes during coition,
how to tell the difference between crow and raven.

Those crows see
our Jupiter, must think it mindless
how we send our probes surfaceward. Send them away,

call them back.
Here are two crows guarding
my sweet basil, watching wasps orbit the one tomato

drooping earthward.
These two crows are exquisite.
They want me to forget about the dumbells hovering

above my head,
to forget about planets.
Two crows call me back from this unpremeditated

meditation
to tell me everything I see
is real save the dark carrion they wait for.

They wait for me
to make a move heavenward
toward them. The sun beats their eyes into mercury.

Depravity
is exquisite. Three crows
reduced to one. One crow to two. One spring

in Italy
the children in the piazza yelled,
Vengono i corvi! The crows are coming. This is how

we learn to love the dark.

The Scarecrow Odes

> I realize at present that I'm only an imitation of a man, and I assure you that it is an uncomfortable feeling to know that one is a fool.
> —Scarecrow, *The Wizard of Oz*

1.

I live at the corner of Beethoven and Schubert.
This is an aesthetic impossibility.

2.

Nixon attended Whittier College, whose team name is The Poets.
Nixon once said, *I am not a crook,* when what he meant was, *I am a Poet.*

3.

Three roads triverged in a yellow wood.
And that makes no difference whatsoever.

4.

I am a metaphor.
I am a metaphor for myself.

5.

One replaces oneself with oneself and an incredible likeness of
    oneself, a likeness so authentic one's very self questions its own
    authenticity. One then begins to refer to oneself as *halfself.*
At each mention of that word, a star flickers, fires full, then burns
    out.

6.

After mowing the lawn barefoot, one finds tiny blood spots on the
driveway. Upon closer inspection, each grass blade is embossed
with J. A. Henckels International. One then realizes that one is
not in the driveway but in the kitchen.
There are chives on the floor. One overripe heirloom tomato has
been hacked open.

7.

The largest encyclopedia of all time was a sixteenth-century
Chinese encyclopedia. It was 22,937 volumes.
The smallest encyclopedia, by comparison, is the left eye of a dying
fly.

8.

One replaces oneself with an effigy of oneself and takes great pains
to give the effigy character. One ultimately fails but sells the
effigy for crossbow practice.
In some religions this is known as sainthood.

9.

Michel Lotito of Grenoble, France has, since 1966, eaten eighteen
bicycles, fifteen supermarket food carts, seven televisions, six
chandeliers, a coffin, and a Cessna airplane. He complains to the
local goatherds that in dreams he is chased by wraith-cyclists in
a flying shopping cart who threaten to make ornamental light
sources of his intestines.
Their eyes are tiny televisions.

10.

Where three roads triverge in a yellow wood a nearby sign reads:
*Three roads triverged in a yellow wood. And that makes no difference
whatsoever.* Underneath, in a scrawling script with which one
might write death threats or last minute grocery lists, someone
has written: *The three roads are a metaphor, which means this sign
is also a metaphor.*
If one were then to look up, a few stars would burn out.

11.

Peace, by definition, is either a state of tranquility or quiet, or a
dying fly on one's window ledge after a night of flurries in
which the birds in the air conditioner fell deathly quiet and all
around the neighborhood German composers and writers and
philosophers rolled over into their names at the same exact
instant the right eye of the fly watched one of the last (one can't
ever know for sure) snowflakes flutter to the ground to be still.
Or it is a state of tranquility.

Scratched Retina: Memento Mori

Dear coffee grounds, ground pepper, memorial crumbs
floor-fallen and pinned there. Dear last night's
doors to heavier sleep through which each eye
feared its twin should wander. Dear wandering
dust in the eye liver-shaped like the shy Brancusi
bust stumbled onto on the internet last night:
forgive this foolish English cottage-style dotage
alive with flies and doorway formicology.
Little fears come in tracks of black ants, brittle
to the touch, skating on the surface of the open eye.
Every eye loves just one lash. And that lash will fall
gravely and unseen like a drachma next to the pound.
Dear dull Drachma: if you died as well, hexed
the very eye you meant to cover well sunken,
would you garner such graven respectability?
Shrill imitator of the crow, in the photo I have, you lie,
still, as in death. Or you are teaching the dead to rest.

Four

Space

I love space.
   —Denis Tito, aboard the *Mir*

1.

In the beginning, when the great mother
ship lands and dishes out its aliens,
who could resist the earthy music, its double

bass, timpani and oboes, those necks
craning out before such rude communion?
And which of us knew then, startled, young

enough to be afraid, that space was, well,
mostly boring? The occasional ping from Earth,
tireprints in moondust, antimatter.

And to reach into the black ink of the new,
strapped comically to a rocket we were
even amused to think of stars somehow

waiting for us to name them, to punctuate
the ends of their lives with a rise in pitch,
odd Latin declension or throaty wisdom

of an Arabic lost even to Arabs.
Love, NASA says, *is an endless stretch
of names for unknown spaces:* some honey-

mooning Jupiter moon, a picture postcard
of the planet Earth, the lunar gray
of a tiny, flawless, human brain.

2.

Enterprise of thousands of confused
Greeks and Romans, lover of the old
typewriter, this space, most likely the last

of the written symbols. And yet we eat
away at the rock wall of it on a page,
or shoot it through with memory's ink and syntax.

Christlike, it will demonstrate
its ribs for doubters. No doubting the italic
S in the white room of its font like

a pharaoh in pyramidal void: living
space loves a spine. Remember before
William Carlos Williams and zip-lock baggies,

the splatter of Gertrude Stein? Now there is space
for everyone and everything in the bright
circle of recycling where we sit

manifest destinied, scalping the words
that filled those long centuries before
the invention of inventing the new

to replace the human. So too the low humors
of a scribe, his quill and muffled cough
in dim lit chambers. There, to think of space

meant one more gilt character or, worse,
a few more graves the size of turnip beds.
And if in the small print of the will of some

Florentine noble's hound, we find the nerve
to use space, what does the *OED*
tell us about the boldness of our world?

It could be sadness, too. This notion of space
being nowhere and endless as our bodies are
floating from one page to the next.

3.

Take any page. Back from Italy,
a month with parents, prying into their lives
in all these rooms. It's sinister really,

the appalling grandeur. And yet for all their space,
mystery jars fall out of the fridge. Bull's-Eye
Barbecue sauce. Last time, boysenberry

preserves. Next, chipotle mayonnaise.
So it is with names for condiments:
as the universe expands, in turn do they.

The garage approximates a Chinese junk
back from the silk road with all the wrong
necessities, its great bay doors shuddering

against the heft of hoarding everything.
Take their movie I love but never see—
It's a Mad Mad Mad Mad World—

that absurd title spinning off its box.
Believe me: you know any generation
by the length of its song and movie titles.

I see how my parents blindly stockpile,
trading word for appliance, deck chair,
salad spice. In Italy, they grinned

at the tiny coffees, the Cokes iceless
and unrefreshing. They watched their two weeks
shrink into a bar corner pocked

with lapdogs, a hushed ash-oasis
finite as the length of their vacation.
Perugia, Assisi: they must have been quietly

constructing their own home along the cobble,
flooring ancient walls, dreaming the air
conditioner could be invented there,

that the apartments Italians called home
would agglomerate, the shells of each
bursting, letting in a little light

for those new, spacious, forgetful houses.
The difference between Europe and the States,
Gigi once told me in the Astrodome,

hot dog cradled in his stifled hands,
the difference is, you believe in the future.
Here, as the cableman fights frogs

out front installing new channels, I hear
the call of atomic physics and repairmen
everywhere: *everything breaks down.*

   4.

Picasso said, *Give me a museum*
and I'll fill it. And I think of him now
as I watch Denis Tito aboard the *Mir,*

how a California speculator
reminds me of the *Man with a Pipe*
fractured through the digital soup of space.

Yet despite cubism, skepticism,
Tito has the sadness of a blue
guitar in the forgiving lap that zero

gravity maintains. A visitor
to our homes, he peers in through news-
papers—a nuisance at first, like the jet-

black lab pup lapping up your bowl
of Cheerios. But I've come to enjoy his Russian
three-day growth, ask myself under

my breath if he's learned any Russian,
if he's eating borscht, and if they'd had
more space, and they'd asked, would I have gone.

And suddenly I'm there among the circuits
and huge views, and I've always been
there. For space, we know, is all matter

of perception. Then my father turns:
That Tito, you have to admit—slapping
his hands down on the leather armrests—

he's a work of art. Why the finger
of the alien throbs on the temple,
why a new house the size of hangar thirteen

will prod us on over the pale dunes
of our more deserted days, more spacious
and comely each square foot we place toward it:

we could explain away every war
and condiment known to humans
as us just wanting to feel better, stronger.

Now that Mars is so much bleaker than Wells
and his *War of the Worlds* wanted us
to know, what use is space? Out there, beyond

the last stand of singed oak, I keep
searching for the end to my parents' rights
as landowners and find only briar,

thick and riddling the treetops. And if I stare
long enough, I can almost feel
each tendril eking out another inch

into our space this side of Earth, some great
buried bulb I picture spindling off,
scrawling up the pined skyline like fingers

on the nape of a genius. I am close
to something here. What did Parisians
want, after all, through the crowd

of Picasso's fingers? Not a dove
or frail horse in a handful of scribbles,
but the master's hand itself. Hovering

above the paper that hand was testament
to its own body of knowledge, as distant
and distinct as the mind that taught it

spatial forms and eating pork in thin strips
without touching the lips. In the end,
what remains are scattered mouthfuls of sound bites,

thumbnail prints, web space with his name
where I'm searching for the quote I used
and come up somehow with his self-portrait

alone in a room of his paintings.
So much communion, fusion in stretched canvas.
A cigarette, here, his surrogate paintbrush.

Millions of years light enough to balance
on a fist of horse-hair opened up.
And now, Denis, NASA, Mother, Father:

tell me why we blast off mouths and rockets
for this unknown space to fill, graffiti-
greedy masons at the wall of becoming.

Rope-hoisted Raphaels in Nero's Golden
House, we're searching for the mossed mosaics,
the expanding farce of our forgetfulness,

when we are the many hands over pages
of an empty score, wandless and cranky,
and poised to forget the lengths the massive

timpani traveled. T minus two seconds.
The living nerves of drumheads test their own
vibrato against the crowd's easy murmur.

Five

All the Ashtrays in Rome

> The popes, I mean in their own way, made a holy water stoup of Rome.
> We Italians, I mean in our own way, have made it into an ashtray.
>   —Pirandello, *The Late Mattia Pascal*

Call it the end of an empire, consumed,
turned by English into a verb: to be
always in the image of the ancient
pilgrimage. You approach the walls, the basin

leading into Ostia still burning
with the memory of Visigoths,
can almost imagine the old roam through
the capital. So unbearable,

the heat from the Coliseum, its scalloped ruins,
Circus Maximus, Hadrian's Mausoleum,
and how they all approximate the ashtray.
You don't even need to be a smoker

to want to find a use for all that ash.
Make it sacred, as Etruscans did.
(Not having cigarettes, they used their dead.)
Or export it to America

in wicker bottles, cardboard funeraries,
memento mori. You'd be Nero-famous.
Like Al Gore smashing federal ashtrays
on TV. Millions listened to him

preach about the government waste inherent
in the glass. Hammer in his hand,
It's not the ashtray I'm against, he said,
the swelling crowds cheering for the blow.

Consider the virtues of the ashtray:
depository of the bleakest moments,
way station for what cannot be
inhaled, digested, given back to Caesar.

For that time after the snuffing out
and the emptying of its bowl, the ashtray
is a continuation of the ascetic
mind. Hell, it could be anywhere.

Who hasn't seen the women crowd around
a cupped palm with a flame inside,
cigarettes reaching out like white tongues.
Or the lone man in the park on Sunday

drifting through the sands of tall ashtrays
for the one half-smoked, his face slowly
pulled into his mouth. There must be days
even he's convinced he's really living

on cigarettes and coffee, which brings us back
to Rome. I've sat in bars and watched the slow
wave of smoke as the door opens again.
I've watched them by the hundreds, cigarettes

resting on their beveled edges, all
the ashtrays in Rome: the seashells put to task,
the bronze, the silver, glass—a history
of western civilization inside each bar.

Though it wasn't always so glamorous.
The day Rome turned to the cult of the living,
ashtrays filled at twice the speed, spilled
onto the counters, shoes, the lapdogs

tied to sinking monuments. The Baths
of Caracalla went dry. Everywhere
the ash kept falling, cigarettes poised
in the manner of Byzantine art:

stiff, long, and usually symbolic.
Come morning ashtrays waited like open mouths.
They teetered on the bar, though the cost
was factored in. Some shattered. Others outlived

their users. What is the misfortune of breaking
ashtrays? Because when it was over,
and the crew swept up, they kept the fragments
for their mantles. To think: our very own vice

president smashing ashtrays. And we
rested well that night, replaying that
ecstatic moment when the hammer fell,
and everyone gasped. And it rained, or we

imagined it rained, crystals, incessantly.
And we awoke in cities made of glass.

The Last Decade of the Fifteenth Century

Meriting slight praise alongside frescoes
still beading perspiration from the hand
laboring there, a century dies.

Few seem particularly interested.
The shepherds pack their bread.
Piazzas fill with beneficent indifference.

Meanwhile the fork appears at dinner,
relegating the hand to other trades:
covering the face; making bread, art.

In Francesco Rosselli's Florentine study
of three candelabra in pen and ink—
brown water coloring, traces

of pencil on white paper—
notice the wide borders and false
starts for a new century. Ten years

and Venice will begin to sink,
enshrined in habitual negligence,
surrounded by sea, colorless.

Florence becomes her own sister,
the less pretty in her perfection.
People are just starting to care

about England. But this is hearsay,
or heresy to the last few years,
the scintillating ones, when everything

seemed possible because everything would end.
Freed from the mighty pencil, figures
flew over the walls of museums

in a manner typifying Greek drama,
fine Swiss watchmanship, or the lazing
over a tourist meal in Venice:

one long, painful meditation
on the inevitable departure of time
from the very hands that created it.

Virtus Dormitiva

Coffee-drunk at a staging of *The Miser,*
I watch him bridge the moat between the blank
stage and first row of chairs with a plank

and walk it, his black robe dragging behind
in tatters, an inquisitor's memory.
Suspended there he seems an inquisitor

to me: a fair-skinned California boy.
You will pay, his finger says, curved
like an amputated question mark,

*pay a miser for the right to see
a miser.* Later at the party I speak
with an ecologist about leeches.

In Indonesia one slouched through the thin
crease of suede on his toe. His shoe answered
by bleeding. And this is not unnatural.

The shoe bleeds because it has been harmed.
The black humor of the shoe: like a leech
on high perch, waiting for the mammal

millennia have taught it walks
underneath. If earthbound, the leeches rise
and sway like tiny theories. Centuries

pass them by untouched, uncharmed mostly
by our taste for the redundant late night
ramble of the scientist in the dark

polo shirt. Not what he says, but how
the words create a vellum around the air
he speaks, how the party in the distance

appears backlit and dizzy, spinning
on the axis of a Saturday
after Molière's miser was the farthest

out, had dropped his gnarled index to gaze
into the invisible sea of the paid
audience. The spotlight discovers his face,

the coiled eyes and horribly jaundiced teeth
of someone so much older than himself.
To me it is a lifetime he stands there

sucking air out of actual lungs.
At intervals, like the imperceptible
turnings of a thought inside the brain,

I watch a thousand hands, white-cuffed,
rise and clash for the charm, the power
to quiet, to sink into the lap, to sleep.

People Who Jump off Cliffs

People who jump off cliffs always have fallen and (as far as we know) will continue to fall, irrespective of what language they spoke or speak.
—Bruce Mitchell and Fred Robinson, *A Guide to Old English,* sixth edition

Distant buoys shimmer in the ocean or lake
over which they stand. If there is no water,
there is no shimmer. Everything remains the same.
Some grief is pain. Some the lack of it.
Which is why if they had it all
over again, they'd still be here, thrown
from their own silhouette the opposite
cliff portrays, beautiful in their frailty,
muddled in churchstone brown and granite
pointillism. I'd like to think of each one
brilliant, an unfolded swan jackknifing
into what a diver learns will translate.
And the entry, like an eye slipping under its lid.

This is wrong. And this is what I mean
by ignorance. Each day I glide across
the river on my bike, ignoring all
the streets that led me there, some tree-lined
and lazy, others rueful. Still others
without any name that I could pin.
Without words. Those must be so golden
to a hungry gorge, nameless itself,
and reason enough to keep me from knowing
how it feels to be a canyon's tongue,
tiny and fretful, with sense enough for one
more word. This then is what translators
know as slippage, words tearing out
of their language and falling into another,
not quite the same. Never quite the same.
Do you see them? They are peering out
from the shores of their new syntax, blithely.
Ignorant of us. And we of them.

Consolation Miracle

> Besides, the few miracles attributed to the angel showed a certain mental disorder, like the blind man who didn't recover his sight but grew three new teeth, or the paralytic who didn't get to walk but almost won the lottery, and the leper whose sores sprouted sunflowers. Those consolation miracles, which were more like mocking fun, had already ruined the angel's reputation when the woman who had been changed into a spider finally crushed him completely.
>
> —García Márquez, "A Very Old Man with Enormous Wings"

In the pewless church of San Juan Chamula,
a neo-Catholic Tzotzil Indian
wrings a chicken's neck. Through piñoned air,
stars from tourist flashbulbs die, reflecting
in each reddened eye, in the mirrors
statuary cling to inside their plate-
glass boxes. A mother fills a shot
glass with fire. Others offer up their moon-
shine swelling in goat bladders, the slender
throats of Coke bottles, as if gods too thirsted
for the real thing. The slightest angle
of a satellite dish sends me to Florida,
where the sleepless claim the stars talk
too much. They stumble to their own
worn Virgin Mary whose eyes, they swear,
bleed. Florida: rising with its dead
even as it sinks into the glade.

Or there, a continent away, the heavenly gait
of Bigfoot in the famous Super 8,
voiced over by a cryptozoologist
who all but laughs at the zipper-lined torso.
Bigfoot trails out of California
into my living room, a miracle
in the muddled middle ground of the event
horizon, in the swell between each seismic wave

where time carries itself like Bigfoot: heavy,
awkward, a touch too real to be real.
And the miracle cleaners make everything
disappear into far too-floral scents.
Miracle-starved, out of sleep or the lack of it,
I keep watching, not to see Bigfoot
but to be Bigfoot, to traipse through screens,
and the countless peering eyes, the brilliant
nebulae bleeding. Yeti, pray
you come again, you Sasquatch. Video
our world for your religions. Memorize
all these pleasure bulbs, these satellites,
our eyes, our stars. Look: how we turn
each other on tonight, one at a time.

Ending

God keep me from ever finishing anything.
  —Melville

My favorite first lines come
—Camus, Tolstoy, Dostoevsky—
    despite translation.
Living near Dallas I see no starting point.
Forgettable scenery stretches like *War*
and Peace in both directions. A hardback,
    in the middle
thousand pages. It is April.
I stop screwing up my year
on checks and forms and settle down,
    balancing blood-
sugar and checkbook—ways I have
to mediate my ever thinking there is no end
to this beginning, that one day I'll wake
    startled in a sun
saffroned by smog, an evening
without night. My friend John writes
from Gothenburg, Sweden. Light, he says,
is the face of God torn away in winter.
John's become ursine. Twenty winters
in Minnesota make him pray to anything
    that gives off heat, light—
the television, computer, last pages of books.
Brown-black cigarette coronas pock his letter
    —*There's your midnight sun*—
as if Sweden turned the world
against him. Light, John, is boring a hole
right through to you, shaking the end
of a stick in your face. Entrenched
in your flat, you're writing a letter to me.
    It ends like this:

Went skating on large lakes glazed with water.
Long skates, and I learned to read ice.
Three hours to cross, only then we turned
back never stopping because stopping
feels like sinking and I never did.
The sky mirrored in the lake surface
and I never stopped. I want to come home.

I think of you now as two rivers
tighten near my house, grumble
old introductions to each other.
Each day I see horizons sliced by the sky.
Endless days, John,
where we begin to notice the darkness,
like a hand, pressing down,
or holding us, the way we hold a book
before closing it.

Other Books in the Crab Orchard Award Series in Poetry

Muse
Susan Aizenberg

This Country of Mothers
Julianna Baggott

White Summer
Joelle Biele

In Search of the Great Dead
Richard Cecil

Names above Houses
Oliver de la Paz

The Star-Spangled Banner
Denise Duhamel

Pelican Tracks
Elton Glaser

Winter Amnesties
Elton Glaser

Fabulae
Joy Katz

Train to Agra
Vandana Khanna

Crossroads and Unholy Water
Marilene Phipps

Misery Prefigured
J. Allyn Rosser

Becoming Ebony
Patricia Jabbeh Wesley